WINE COUNTRY
TRUCKS
of NAPA & SONOMA COUNTIES

Published by Wine Country Trucks Publishing
Second Printing Special Edition July 2015

ISBN # 978-0-9913530-3-3

Books may be purchased at:
www.winecountrytrucks.com

Correspondence or orders to:
info@winecoutrytrucks.com

Photography, Text and Maps by Lisa A. Harris
Editing by Keri Brenner
Book Design by Zoe Lonergan

Printed in China

WINE COUNTRY
TRUCKS

of NAPA & SONOMA COUNTIES

Photography and Text

by

LISA A. HARRIS

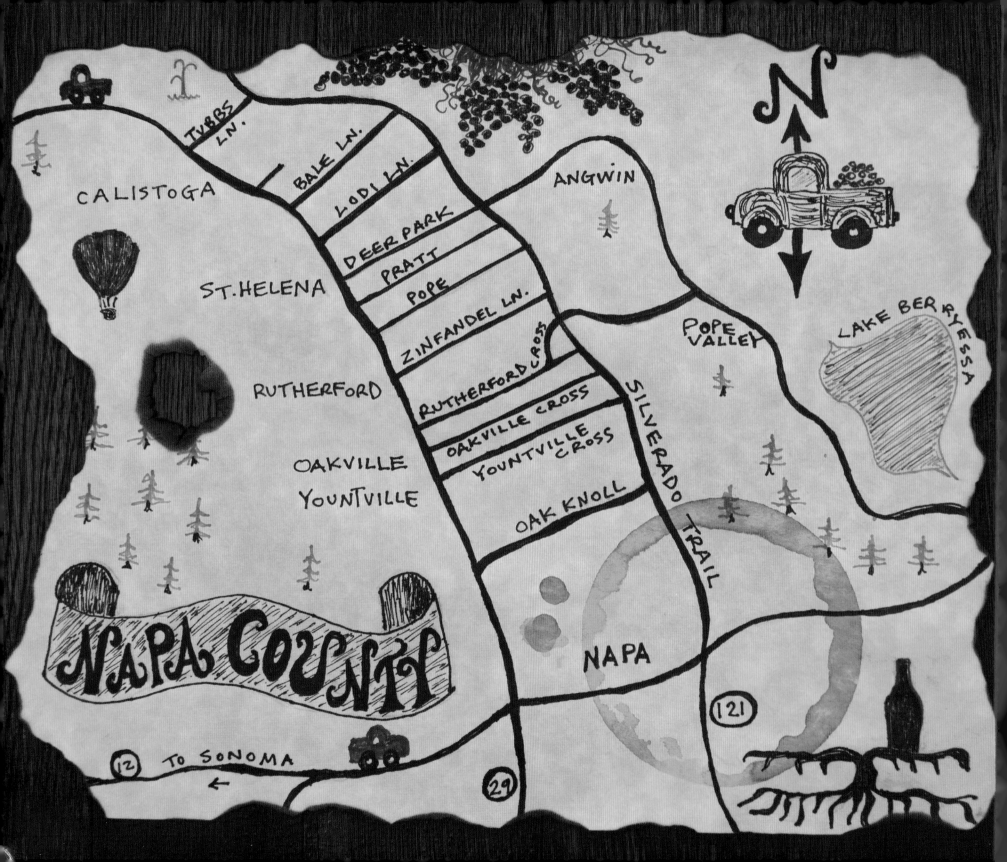

CONTENTS

iv   Napa County Map

1   Foreword

NAPA COUNTY

5   Napa

25   Oakville

37   Rutherford

47   St. Helena

63   Calistoga

71   Pope Valley

SONOMA COUNTY

79   Sonoma

91   Glen Ellen

101   Santa Rosa

111   Fulton

117   Windsor

123   Healdsburg

143   Sonoma County Map

144   Wine Country Listings

147   Parts

150   Acknowledgements

FOREWORD

From the grape-clustered rows of Napa, through the golden oak-sprinkled hills of Alexander Valley, along the curves of Dry Creek, to sunny Sonoma and beyond, I've scoured the Northern Wine Country of California in search of the sometimes-elusive Wine Country Truck.

This is a collection of timeless treasures, relics of the past. Some are proudly presented, while others are sentenced to weedy fields or the silence of wrecking yards. Yet, all evoke the need to reminisce of bygone days, of simpler times, of an America innocent. It was a time of homemade apple pie, county fairs, black and white T.V. and nighttime games of kick the can. To each owner, the memories are dear and held close to the heart like an old friend. Some worked tirelessly in the vines hauling decades of grapes. Others delivered wine, loaded plums and apples or simply taught a child driver propped on a tattered pillow, reaching to see over the steering wheel.

In many cases, it was possible to uncover histories of these beasts of burden, these time machines. Through lengthy interviews, sheer determination and sometimes mild pestering, I was able to discover their untold stories.

For others, it was not to be. If only they could talk, years of stories could be told. They'd reveal times of happiness, sorrow, triumph, defeat, loves lost and found, children born and parents passing. Legends could be learned, but those secrets will remain locked in the cabs of these old trucks, these trusted friends. Imagination is our vehicle to travel the road to yesteryear.

My hope is for each page to lead you down a memory lane with a smile and a feeling that warms the heart and feeds the soul.

Now buckle up! It's time to do some time traveling.

NAPA COUNTY

—————◆—————

ARTESA VINEYARDS AND WINERY

UPTOWN THEATRE

NAPA

Bouchaine Vineyards

Carneros Region

Laird Family Estate Winery

Napa Marina

Regusci Winery

Reynolds Family Winery

Road 31 Wine Company

Robinson Family Vineyards

V12 Vineyards

BOUCHAINE VINEYARDS

"Sold!" "To Gerret and Tatiana Copeland!" Those were the auctioneer's words back in 1998, when the owners of Bouchaine Winery won the last and final bid at the annual Napa Valley Vintners Wine Auction. It was like music to their ears.

Not only were they awarded the well-worn '54 Chevy pickup, but they also received a truck bed full of assorted elite premium Napa Valley wines too.

The old timer was then refurbished to its current pristine condition. Today, the shining Chevy is driven for novelty appearances – such as the Napa Fourth of July parade or promotional events. In the interim, many hours are spent basking in sunshine at the Bouchaine tasting room, solely for the pleasure it gives to the guests.

CARNEROS REGION

Most of the life of this 1929 National Series was spent slaving away in the orchards and hay fields in the Carneros region of Napa. It was the first truck Chevrolet built and sold with a six-cylinder engine. In 1962, it was sold to the Schwarze family, also of Carneros.

For over fifty years, this old hay hauler has remained posted as a sentry, overseeing the vineyards and enduring the seasons.

LAIRD FAMILY ESTATE WINERY

Like a lone pioneer, it made the cross-country trip from East Coast to West.

The Laird family purchased this 1931 Ford Model A pickup from a relative in upstate New York in 2008 and had it trucked all the way to Napa! That relative had bought it twelve years prior and spent about $800 in work and tires. Everything on this Model A is original, except the side boards, which were added to make it Laird Family Estate Winery's official winery truck. It has never been restored. It even came with the 1931 owner's manual!

On weekends, it is proudly showcased at the winery entrance, adjacent to Highway 29 near the Oak Knoll crossing. It drives perfectly.

NAPA MARINA

Commonly known as the "Marina" truck, this 1954 Chevy half-ton pickup marks the first year of the automatic pickup truck. It is owned by a marina resident who, for the past six years, has parked it under the same familiar palm. Instead of side boards, he used oars for racks, which seems to encourage smiles and waves wherever he goes.

REGUSCI WINERY

Gaetano Regusci purchased this 1926 White truck new as one of eleven vehicles needed to operate the Regusci Ranch. Beginning in the early 1930s, its occupation was delivering fresh milk and ranch-raised beef to customers throughout the Napa Valley.

The White Motor Company antique pickup is a revered family artifact on exhibit at the historic Regusci Winery, located in the Stags Leap District of Napa.

REYNOLDS FAMILY WINERY

At the southern end of the Napa Valley on Silverado Trail is the casually elegant Reynolds Family Winery. Parked to the left of the driveway leading to their tasting room is one sleek, black 1952 International Harvester truck.

Steve and Suzie Reynolds first spotted it when their friend and client, Jack Daniels (not that Jack Daniels), a Wilson Daniels wine distributor, drove the '52 pickup to Reynolds Family Winery to blend wine with Steve. Steve told him, "If you ever sell it, give me the first call." One day, Jack appeared with the truck at the Reynolds Family Winery to deliver it to Steve as a special gift from his loving wife Suzie.

From the outside, the Harvester looks original and is beautifully restored to the time period. On the inside, you'll find a Corvette engine, automatic adjusting seats and remote entry.

ROAD 31 WINE COMPANY

Over submarine sandwiches in a modest Kansas diner, Kent Fortner listened to his grandmother Mary tell the story of the green '66 Ford pickup parked outside the restaurant window. Kent made the cross-country trip to retrieve the green truck willed to him by his grandfather, a Kansas farmer.

Mary explained how at the age of sixteen, her mother had arranged a date with a fella from a city in southern Kansas. Back then, communication wasn't so good. When Mary arrived, her "would-be" date was out working the four-state, wheat harvest loop. His parents assigned her to a chaperone whose name was Loren. He would later become

Kent's grandfather. Mary wove a beautiful story of separation, love letters lost and love found. In 1937, Mary and Loren were married. They bought the truck new in 1966. Loren vowed one day to take his bride on a honeymoon to Niagara Falls. Finally, in 1982, packed in their favorite green pickup, they made the promised trip.

Four years later, at that little Kansas diner, Kent's grandmother handed him the keys. Right then and there, he'd found the name and artwork for his winery. It would be Road 31 Wine Company, with the green truck pictured on the label. Road 31 connected the homesteads of both sets of Kansas grandparents. If you were to let the truck drive itself, to Road 31 it would go.

ROBINSON FAMILY VINEYARDS

Hidden atop a gentle hillside on the east side of Silverado Trail in Napa is Robinson Family Vineyards. You can spot this flashy blue 1937 Ford flatbed pickup angled beside their private tasting room doors. It still has a flathead V8-85 horsepower motor. Only 800 pickups had that flatbed.

On occasion, it can be seen frequenting its favorite Yountville restaurants or in a local parade with grandkids throwing candy and waving from the bed.

V12 VINEYARDS

V12 signifies several different things. "V" represents the Vasser family who own a local automotive business. Twelve was Jimmy Vasser Jr.'s winning number when he won the Indy Car Championship in 1996. His KV Racing Technology team won the Indy 500 in 2013. The ultimate racing engine is also known as a V12. In addition, the twelve stands for four vineyard blocks with four clones planted on four different rootstocks.

The handsome centerpiece of the Vasser Vineyards is one extraordinary two-tone 1950 Chevrolet pickup truck. Its purpose is to grace hometown parades, local events and to radiate joy. Still in its original stock form and immaculate condition, the vintage Chevy often daydreams of hearing those anticipated "Indy" words: "Gentlemen, start your engines!"

FAR NIENTE WINERY

OAKVILLE

Far Niente Winery

Nickel & Nickel Winery

Oakville Pump Service

Turnbull Wine Cellars

FAR NIENTE WINERY

Beth and Gil Nickel discovered this 1950 Chevrolet panel truck in 1991 and took it to award-winning restorer Phil Cool. His magic transformed the vehicle into an exquisite masterpiece that can be seen delivering good wine and cheer throughout the Napa Valley.

NICKEL & NICKEL WINERY

One of the most photographed trucks in the Napa Valley is Nickel & Nickel's 1929 Ford Model AA. It was purchased in 2003 to add to the farmstead appeal of the property and to honor the vision of the nineteenth century proprietor, John Sullenger.

OAKVILLE PUMP SERVICE

Twenty-some odd years ago on a property north of Trancas Street and east of Big Ranch Road in Napa, two old well drilling rigs sat cloaked in a bramble of blackberry bushes. The berry vines had slowly inched into the empty cabs, climbed onto rounded hoods and snaked completely around both passive, rusted bodies. For decades, this drilling pair remained undetected and engulfed in a sea of green, dotted with deep purple by summer's end. That is, until the property changed hands.

The owner of Oakville Pump Service got a call from a buddy who was asked to remove the neglected duo. The buddy chose his favorite and offered the other to the Oakville Pump owner. Ever since the blackberry bush rescue, this '40s International has become a permanent monument in the southwest corner of the Oakville Pump parking lot. Sometimes tourists can be seen posing for pictures alongside the truck. Once in a while on top of it! It is believed this notorious well driller dug many a well in the Napa Valley during the '50s and '60s.

TURNBULL
WINE CELLARS

Not only is Turnbull known for its world class gallery featuring photographic masters, it is also famous for two classic vehicles parked daily outside the tasting room and garden.

The first parking space in the lot features this shiny crimson '47 Ford half-ton pickup, recently restored by a family member. The deep red hue was inspired by the turning bull graphic on the wine label. Although it has been in the family for generations, it was acquired by Turnbull's owner for his love of antique trucks and never used to do winery labor.

TURNBULL WINE CELLARS

As you meander through the trellis-covered walkway toward the Turnbull tasting room, you'll discover this genuine 1928 Ford AA containing all its original parts.

Turnbull's owner purchased it twenty-five years ago from a once-bustling Nebraska lumberyard with the intention of offering the Ford a comfortable retirement plan at the winery. Now it soaks up the Napa Valley sunshine, promotes fine Cabernet and treats curious visitors to a bit of old fashioned eye candy.

PEJU PROVINCE WINERY

RUTHERFORD

Fleury Estate Winery

Frog's Leap Winery

Round Pond Estate Winery

Rutherford Grove Winery

FLEURY ESTATE WINERY

At the very dead end of a quiet country road in St. Helena, behind a large swinging wooden gate, is the picturesque Fleury Estate. Protected by outstretched oaks are hilly vineyards, cozy cabins and one unusual '30s GMC flatbed backed into its final parking place. History of the truck is not known. However, the twenty-eight acre ranch was purchased circa 1908 with a single gold coin worth $10. It remained a working family ranch until the Fleurys took ownership through a probate sale more than ten years ago. They have transformed the old walnut orchard into fifteen acres of high yielding Cabernet Sauvignon grapes which are processed at their winery in Rutherford.

FROG'S LEAP WINERY

Driven every day by Frog's Leap winemaker and owner John Williams, this classic 1969 Chevy pickup is a familiar sight around the vineyards in Rutherford. Its entire life has been spent in the Napa Valley. Its first years were at the service of a local contractor. The last twenty have been at Frog's Leap Winery, helping to bring in the crop.

ROUND POND ESTATE WINERY

Back in 2003, a Vietnam War veteran sold this 1941 Chevrolet half-ton pickup to Bob McDonnell, owner of Round Pond Estate Winery & Olive Mill. Because Bob was about the same age as the truck, he didn't have the heart to see it go to the junkyard. What he didn't realize, when he purchased it over the phone, was that it lay in tiny pieces on an oil-soaked cement floor.

Through the capable hands and dedicated perseverance of Lonnie, Round Pond Winery's "go to" fix-it-all person for more than twenty years, the mission was accomplished. Lonnie had assembled an expert team to reconstruct the parted pickup to its original glory. Once restored, Bob painted it fire engine red! During a subsequent trip around the vineyard with his son, the steering wheel dropped off in his hands. Luckily, no harm was done. By day, it is situated between a patch of giant agaves and a vineyard row, gracing the majestic palm-lined entrance to the winery, greeting all who enter.

RUTHERFORD GROVE WINERY

Up in the eastern hills of the Napa Valley lies the sleepy town of Angwin. It was home to this 1927 Chevy until a ranch sale was held about thirty years ago. Owners of the Rutherford Grove Winery made a package offer at the sale that included farm equipment, tools and two vehicles. This four-cylinder Chevy truck with a honeycombed radiator and wooden steering wheel was one of the two.

After hauling their ranch treasures home, the new owners treated the little Chevy to a fresh set of tires, a battery, gas and oil. It started right up! Because they enjoy the rustic appearance of the truck, it has never been restored and is used for special occasions at Rutherford Grove Winery.

BERINGER FRONTAGE

ST. HELENA

Benessere Vineyards

Bremer Family Winery

Flora Springs Winery

Long Meadow Ranch Winery

Rossi Vineyard

V. Sattui Winery

BENESSERE VINEYARDS

If you are heading north from the lively town of St. Helena, you might find your foot suddenly hitting the brake pedal when you reach Big Tree Road. Not only is it home to Benessere Vineyards, but also to this magnificent cherry red Mercury stationed out front.

Ford Motor Company of Canada manufactured this 1950 Mercury pickup. It consists of a basic 1950 Ford, but it is built to Canadian specifications, and is very rare. In addition, compliance with Mercury specifications required obtaining obscure parts to make it authentic. John Benish, owner of Benessere Winery purchased this vehicle from the original restorer about twelve years ago. It has been maintained in its original condition. Approximately 3,700 of these trucks were produced.

Usually parked at the western edge of the property on Highway 29, it has become a well known landmark and an iconic winery truck.

BREMER FAMILY WINERY

A California vineyard with deep generational roots was the first home of this 1936 Ford flatbed. It was used in this family-owned vineyard for over fifty-five years and eventually sold in an estate auction. Twenty-three years ago, John Bremer purchased the flatbed at auction and had it fully refurbished. It currently functions as a working truck at the Bremer Family Winery.

Its off time is spent backed into its home – a custom white pillared shed and launch pad, surrounded by mighty oaks on the slopes of Howell Mountain at Bremer Family Winery.

FLORA SPRINGS WINERY

Perched on a knoll at the base of the Mayacamas Mountains on the Flora Springs Estate, rests this well-worn 1937 International flatbed. It was obtained in Nevada to enhance the ambiance of the Flora Springs tasting room frontage.

The name Flora honors the beloved mother and grandmother who saw the magic hidden behind decades of neglect when she first laid eyes on the abandoned ghost winery more than thirty years ago.

"Springs" refers to the natural springs on the property that have flowed uninterrupted, even through periods of drought. As the springs, Flora's spirit will flow for generations to come.

LONG MEADOW RANCH WINERY

This old green '48 Ford F-2 pickup belonged to Fred Bertolini. He did odd jobs for the Halls at Long Meadow Ranch and he always drove his truck (sometimes with his wife, who would come along to pick blackberries and later make them a pie). Ted Hall had a standing joke with Fred. Every time he saw Fred he'd say, "I want to buy your truck." Fred would always reply, "She's mine and she's not for sale."

Fred bought the pickup new in '48. He drove her everywhere and always kept her spotless. He added chrome wheels, but everything else was original. Everyone in town knew it was Fred's truck.

When Fred passed unexpectedly, Ted struggled with getting up the nerve to call Fred's wife about the truck. Not long afterwards, Ted was driving his family to a Fourth of July parade in Calistoga. Alongside the road was Fred's truck decked out in red, white and blue balloons with a "For Sale" sign in the window! Ted nearly wrecked the car. He stopped and ran back to the truck to confirm what he already knew. It *was* Fred's truck.

The family was anxious to get to the parade. Ted relented and continued on to the Fourth festivities, but he couldn't get his mind off the truck. The minute they returned home, Ted was

on the phone to Fred's wife, Lois. Ted told her not to sell it. He'd be there in the morning. As he drove up the driveway the following day, they both cried. They went into garage where Lois placed some of Fred's tools on the front seat of the truck. When Ted asked her how much (a lot), he said, "done." There was no dickering on the price.

That was in 1996. The truck has been a fixture at Long Meadow Ranch and the St. Helena Farmers' Market ever since. In 1998, the local dealer, Zumwalt Ford, proudly posted a picture of Fred's truck in their showroom to honor the 50th anniversary of Ford F-Series trucks.

ROSSI VINEYARD

Arthur Rossi, eldest son and winemaker for the Rossi Family Vineyard, purchased this Chevy pickup new in 1950. It resides in its original home on the fifty-two acre parcel along Highway 29, commonly known as the Rossi Ranch and now owned by Frog's Leap Winery.

In 2010, working closely with the Land Trust of Napa County, Frog's Leap inspired a conservation easement on this iconic farm, ensuring the rural character of the landscape and the Rossi history are preserved into perpetuity. As if a symbol, the old Rossi relic is a reminder of how honoring the past can enhance the future and become an integral part of the present. Home is where the truck is.

V. SATTUI WINERY

Yop Tepping, a Swedish immigrant farmer living in St. Helena, purchased this '45 Chevy flatbed at the end of the military production lines. The truck was his pride and joy.

In the late '40s, early '50s, during prune harvest season, Yop would gather the three local Talcott children, hoist them onto the flatbed and head to his orchard in Rutherford. On their knees, the children would harvest the prunes into fifty-pound lug boxes. When the truck was fully stacked, Yop carted them back to the prune dehydrator in St. Helena.

Many years later, after schooling and military service, Dr. James Talcott returned to St. Helena. When he and his partner purchased the Dowdell Lane property, there sat an abandoned derelict '45 Chevy. Low and behold, it was the same truck he'd picked prunes from as a child!

Over the next several years, it was restored to mint condition. Ironically, the restorer, Russ Aves, lives on Yop's old property. For thirty-three years, the flatbed was stored in a barn. In 2011, it took on the job of transporting olives and Talcott Carneros Olive Oil. Due to impatient California drivers, the slow-going, loaded truck was not welcomed on the busy highways. Hence, "sold" to V. Sattui Winery!

Now parked adjacent to the winery, it sports banners announcing upcoming events and winery milestones.

V. SATTUI WINERY

For many years, this worn and weathered '46 Chevy flatbed was on the clock and part of the winemaking team. It was used to haul grape pomace, tow gondolas and transport pallets of wine between the winery and a case-good warehouse across the street. Dario Sattui bought the sturdy flatbed from his neighbors back in 1977.

Now lounging in idle seclusion at the southern end of V. Sattui Winery, its running board props the faded sign, "Voted Best Winery in the Western U.S. 2005 Critics Challenge."

Dario was also the visionary behind the creation of Castello di Amorosa Winery in Calistoga. Many enthusiastic tourists are shuttled between the two popular locations and have enjoyed the nostalgic presence of both classic Chevys situated in V. Sattui's vineyard in St. Helena.

CHATEAU MONTELENA WINERY

CALISTOGA

Lava Vine Winery

Tank Garage Winery

Tractor Parade

Trailside Inn

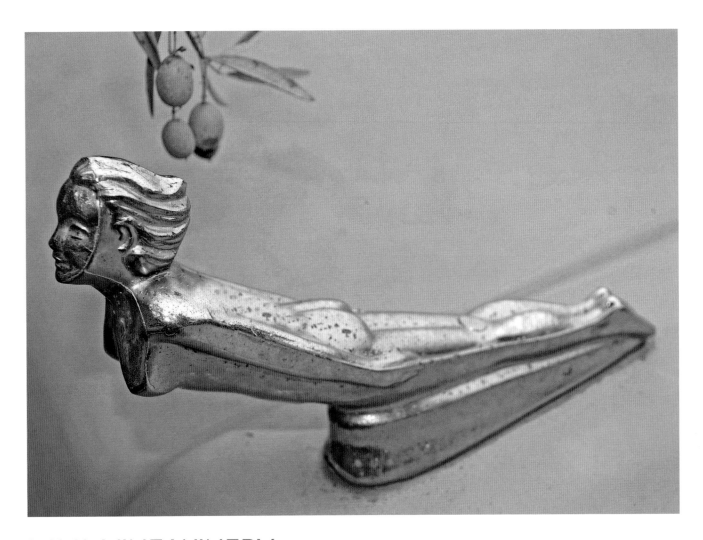

LAVA VINE WINERY

Since this old gold 1971 Ford pickup was purchased new from the dealer, it has been a respected family friend. With the addition of a stout camper mounted on the bed, it toured the Cabral family all over the country and Canada on memorable and scenic summer vacations. In 2012, it was kindly passed from father to son. Now, as a member of the winery crew, this willing worker hauls equipment and faithfully patrols the vineyards. Lava Vine Winery will be its forever home.

TANK GARAGE WINERY

Reminiscent of a '30s-era gas station along Route 66, Tank Garage Winery in Calistoga is the vision of two lifelong friends. After decades of collective farming experience and world-class winemaking, they decided to celebrate the heart and soul of California culture and creativity. They refurbished the dilapidated gas station which was fully operational from the 1930s to the 1980s. It now serves as their tasting room where hand-crafted wines are poured.

On occasion, the 1928 Ford Model A represents the winery. It is owned by an old friend who received the Ford as a birthday gift from his son. The son bought it in Oregon from a lucky gambler who'd won it in a poker game!

At the heart of Tank Garage Winery is the notion that ideas and influences continually surround us, tease us and tempt us. Whether you're facing the new, the unknown or honoring the past – hold onto it and embrace it. Above all …. Never Dream Alone.

TRACTOR PARADE

During the Christmas season, the Calistoga Chamber of Commerce sponsors the annual Calistoga Lighted Tractor Parade to honor the agricultural heritage of their community. This quirky, small-town celebration presents tractors, antique trucks and construction equipment decked in twinkling streamers of holiday lights. Rain or shine, they parade down the charming main street of Calistoga for the enjoyment of locals and tourists alike.

TRAILSIDE INN

In the heart of Calistoga, tucked between vineyards and well-traveled wineries, is the Trailside Inn, a charming 1930s farmhouse. Sprawling lawns, plentiful gardens and vineyard sunsets accompany this native Ford, known as Old Blue. It was acquired locally by the owners of Trailside Inn twenty years ago.

Looks can be deceiving, as is true for Old Blue. The original motor was replaced by a big-block 396 Chevy motor, a TH400 transmission was installed and it was given a new front end. Old Blue is actually a 1949 Ford F-3 and considered very rare. This muscle truck is way too tough to buff!

POPE VALLEY

Pope Valley Garage

Pope Valley Repair & Towing

POPE VALLEY GARAGE

Even though this 1949 or '50 Chevy dump truck is parked in Brad Kirkpatrick's wrecking yard in Pope Valley, it isn't retired. From 1949 to 1964, it was used as a utility vehicle on the 1,300-acre Kirkpatrick turkey and cattle ranch. Mainly, it trucked turkey manure out of sheds that housed thirty five thousand turkeys. But it also hauled fence posts, wire, wood and feed.

Currently, its job is cleaning out silt from the lake behind the wrecking yard. A metal plate was welded onto the front bumper. In case the truck ever got stuck, a hook could be set into the plate for a tow that wouldn't damage the front end.

The combination of headlights, grill and the metal tongue plate create a comical expression of a face grinning at its rusty tractor companions.

POPE VALLEY GARAGE

Oroville, California got a GMC truck and Pope Valley became the new home to this 1923 Mack truck. Brad Kirkpatrick, owner of Pope Valley Garage, made the straight across trade twenty-five years ago. Back then, this Mack had a winch and it ran. As an avid collector of old trucks and tractors, Brad didn't care to drive it. He added the truck to his extensive collection and it has been parked in the same sunny wrecking yard spot ever since.

POPE VALLEY REPAIR & TOWING

Cut! Take two! Those were familiar words to this 1928 Moreland truck back in 1960. Walt Disney used it on the set of his family western, "Pollyanna," starring Haley Mills and filmed in St. Helena. Upon movie completion, the truck was cast to the local Chevy dealer and later to the St. Helena High agricultural department.

Brad Kirkpatrick spotted it stored next to the school's Quonset hut and knew he had to have the old movie prop. He was able to encourage a sale, but only after a thirty-day bid process. In the end, no one met Brad's $35 bid and he drove the old Moreland home to Pope Valley.

Two years ago, Jeff Parady of Pope Valley Repair became the rightful owner. Although it is now yard décor, Jeff is still very "Pollyanna" about his famous truck.

POPE VALLEY REPAIR & TOWING

From ice trucker to school bus, this 1919 Ford Model T changed its vocation in the late '20s when it was given to the school in Calistoga by Union Ice Company. At that time, a homemade bus body was constructed to house the children and shuttle them between their farms and school.

In later years, the old Ford was a regular Calistoga parade-goer, but it eventually became "the little engine that couldn't." Rescued by Calistogan and historian Kurt Larrecou, the old ice truck was fondly passed to its final owner at Pope Valley Repair.

SONOMA COUNTY

ST. FRANCIS WINERY & VINEYARDS

CORNERSTONE SONOMA

SONOMA

Fremont Diner

Gundlach Bundschu Winery

Lovall Valley Vineyards

Sonoma Creamery

Sorento Imports

FREMONT DINER

About six years ago, this '54 International Harvester R-110 longbed pickup resided in Burbank, California where it was used as a prop on a movie set. Unfortunately for the producers, the movie flopped and all the props were to be sold, including the truck. Fortunately for the owner of the Fremont Diner, he learned of the impending sale. This was to be the perfect mascot for his newly acquired retro diner. Because the production company adhered to strict insurance guidelines, the truck was in absolute perfect working order.

After the sale, the Harvester was driven up to its new home in Sonoma. It was then wet sanded to bring out the original patina colors and clear coated to prevent further rusting. The pig logo was hand painted on the doors and now appears on stacks of T-shirts inside the diner. Besides serving as the diner mascot, the longbed is used for catering and can be spotted at the local farmers' market

The Fremont Diner is more than a throwback from the past. It's a place where serious Southern food is done with distinction. One of the favorites is fried chicken over waffles. Most ingredients are from the farm out back and the rest are gathered from nearby friends.

GUNDLACH BUNDSCHU WINERY, RHINEFARM ESTATE VINEYARD

Because Gundlach Bundschu Winery (locally known as Gun Bun) is the oldest family-owned winery in California, it logically has one of the oldest winery trucks.

Walter Bundschu (third generation of Gundlach Bundschu Winery), used this 1927 Chevrolet one-ton to haul grapes, oats, hay and pears to market. It was the only truck of its size on the ranch until a second one arrived in 1947. At that time, Walter's son Towle sawed off the top of the cab so that it could be driven through the orchard and below the limbs of the pear trees. This allowed fruit to be harvested directly into the bins that lined the truck bed.

Jim Bundschu's first driving experience was in 1955, when his father, Towle, instructed him to drive across a field littered with baled hay and to avoid the bales, which he mostly did.

The aging Chevy's last trip off of Rhinefarm was in 1966 when Jim delivered two tons of pears to the Vineburg delivery yard about a mile away. He parked the old jalopy on the ranch. Since that day, it was never driven again.

LOVALL VALLEY VINEYARDS

Sonoma's Lovall Valley has been home to this 1927 Ford Roadster for its entire life. Sold or traded between several owners, it has hauled turkeys, hay, feed and everything associated with farming and ranching.

During prohibition, the Lovall Valley had a thriving moonshine industry. Some said bootleggers were as common as coyotes. This runner is said to have made many a moonlit ride on the back roads of Napa and Sonoma under the cloak of darkness, headlights off.

In 2005, Jim Stroupe bought the roadster and its colorful history with a Lovall Valley property. He continues to drive it as a working ranch machine — minus the moonshine.

SONOMA CREAMERY

In 1931, during the depths of the Great Depression, amidst rich pasture land and vibrant vineyards, Sonoma Creamery was founded. This 1931 Ford AA one-and-a-half-ton flatbed is a replica of the truck used by the original creamery for transporting milk and cheese. Eighty-two years later, Sonoma Creamery still produces small batches of fine artisan cheeses, although now its distribution is a good deal larger than this truck can manage on its own.

In 1997, the grandson and great-grandson of Sonoma Creamery's co-founder drove this very truck in the MBNA XV Great Race. Backed by the enthusiasm of the entire town of Sonoma, they embarked on an incredible journey across Middle America's back roads in this '31 Ford, never exceeding the speed of forty-five miles per hour. After 4,200 miles, they reached the Jacksonville, Florida finish line for what became a father and son's trip of a lifetime.

SORENTO IMPORTS

A chicken farmer from El Verano, which is now part of the city of Sonoma, was the first owner of this 1926 Ford Model T pickup. The farmer used it to haul poultry and eggs to the nearby city of Sonoma, selling to merchants in the town plaza. In 1944, a young teenager named Jim McKenna purchased the pickup for $20. His father told him he paid too much. If Jim didn't get it cleaned up and presentable looking within a week, his father said, he would have to sell it. Jim abided, and proceeded to drive it for many years. He made regular trips to Napa to attend college and even ventured to Fresno, about a 400-mile round trip! After seventy years of ownership, Jim decided to sell the tired truck.

Recently, the Grimms, owners of Sorrento Imports and Café Scooteria in Sonoma, purchased the old Tin Lizzie. They have it on display and in use at their store. The Model T is once again a commercial service vehicle and a rolling part of Sonoma history.

Jim McKenna comes around regularly to keep a "man eye" on his old truck.

B.R. COHN WINERY

GLEN ELLEN

Beltane Ranch

Benziger Family Winery

B.R. Cohn Winery

Glen Lyon Winery

Mayo Family Winery

BELTANE RANCH

Affectionately known as Old Yeller, this 1953 Chevrolet 3100 Series pickup has been an old friend on Beltane Ranch for decades. It was left to the family by a very close friend.

Old Yeller was the first manual transmission vehicle to teach the kids in the family how to drive.

It can be seen regularly as a prop in photos for LL Bean, Pendleton, Woolrich, William Sonoma and NapaStyle.

This working ranch and quaint bed and breakfast is home to six generations who carry on the traditions of growing grapes, fruit, vegetables, olives and raising grass fed beef. Abundant floral gardens surround and oaks embrace this colorful place Old Yeller calls home.

BENZIGER FAMILY WINERY

Nestled on Sonoma Mountain, amongst gently rolling vineyards, is the Benziger Family Winery, specializing in biodynamic farming. One young family member has an extracurricular specialty — hot rodding.

Originally, this 1948 Diamond-T 404 was owned by Rooks Brothers House Moving in Eugene, Oregon. It was rebuilt by Buck Benziger. The cab was installed on a newer one-ton frame with a Detroit diesel twin-turbo 453-T. The transmission is an Eaton Fuller RT-6610, backed by a three-speed auxiliary transmission. It was built outside (the hard way), with old-time trucking style in mind. Now reconstructed, it is one lean, mean, grape-hauling machine.

B.R. COHN WINERY

Shipped new to Manila in the Philippines, this 1946 Ford Woody served the U.S. Embassy after World War II until 1986. Restored by local craftsmen in the Philippines using Philippine mahogany, this vintage Woody wagon has been re-sided and repainted. It was recently refitted with a new Corvette LS2 engine, automatic 6-speed transmission and a Mustang rack-and-pinion front end suspension. With the exception of a few squeaks, it drives like new. Since its restoration, this Woody has been owned by Bruce R. Cohn, founder of B.R. Cohn Winery.

While studying broadcasting and communications in the '60s, Bruce became intimately involved in the San Francisco music scene. It was a heyday for great music. Bruce and his younger brother Martin were often found at the many up and coming nightclubs and bars which today are known to have spurred the careers of many rock 'n' roll legends.

It was around this time in 1970 that Bruce met and became manager of the Doobie Brothers. He helped them climb the charts, catapulting them into rock 'n' roll stardom and is still their manager today.

Every year, Bruce brings his passion of wine and music together during the Sonoma Music Festival produced by B.R. Cohn Charity Events. Wine lovers and music fans flock to this annual event to revel in the beauty of Wine Country while listening to top musical acts. As their song says, "Wo, oh, listen to the music!"

GLEN LYON WINERY

Taking a snooze before the next work day, this '54 Chevy pickup is used like a workhorse during harvest at the Glen Lyon Winery, snuggled between hillside vineyards in the Glen Ellen countryside.

MAYO FAMILY WINERY

At the age of sixteen, Jeffrey Mayo was given this 1931 Chevrolet pickup by his father, who was in real estate at the time. His father had a client who sold some land and couldn't afford to pay him a real estate commission in cash. Instead, the client paid with five vehicles: a Rolls-Royce, a Lincoln Continental, an Austin, a Ford Fairlane and the Chevy truck that didn't run.

Jeffrey took the broken-down pickup to Piner High – his high school in Santa Rosa. In auto shop class, he took it completely apart and carefully pieced the truck back together to working order. He later had it painted and upholstered. It has the original six-cylinder, 24-horsepower engine.

Today, the restored Chevy sits contentedly in front of the Mayo Family Winery tasting room, joins the Kenwood Fourth of July parade or appears in the Glen Ellen fall parade.

MATANZAS CREEK WINERY

SANTA ROSA

———————————————————

Annadel Estate Winery

D'Argenzio Winery

Hook & Ladder Winery

Paradise Ridge Winery

ANNADEL ESTATE WINERY

In the far western corner of Sonoma Valley, beneath massive oaks, in a living storybook, lies the hidden gem – Annadel Estate Winery. Dozing beside its historic barn naps one fine yellow ride.

Owned by Dean Bordigioni, this classic 1955 Chevy is a perfect original. Restoration and genius hot rodding were done by Absolute Customs in Petaluma. Nicknamed "'55 Gorgeous," this "sleeper" looks primarily stock on the outside, but everything underneath is a custom, full-blown hot rod. It is a working winery truck, except for the real dirty jobs.

D'ARGENZIO WINERY

Positioned at the forefront of D'Argenzio's Italian-flavored winery and tasting room is one heavy-duty 1940 Chevy flatbed vintage grape hauler. It was purchased in the Old Santa Rosa Winery District. St. Peter's Ranch was the original owner.

HOOK &
LADDER WINERY

Although the history of this 1961 Willys Jeep is difficult to verify, it is believed that originally it was built for service at New Jersey's McGuire Air Force base.

These Jeeps were used as crash vehicles at Thule Air Force Base in Greenland. It may have serviced a manned emergency landing strip in Greenland, possibly Station Nord. Nord was used by the United States Air Force in conjunction with the Royal Danish Air Force, for re-supply operations — code named "Brilliant Ice." Station Nord closed for two years in 1972. It is possible the Jeep was then returned to its home base in New Jersey.

During the '70s, it was used by the Berkeley Heights, New Jersey volunteer fire department. Eventually, the Willys was retired and sold to a California collector.

In 2001, Cecil De Loach, founder of De Loach Vineyards and Hook & Ladder Winery, was alerted by his mechanics of the available Jeep fire

truck in need of restoration. Being a retired fireman and an avid restorer of American cars and trucks, he purchased the Willys Jeep. With precise attention to detail, a complete frame-off restoration was performed and finished in 2005.

Today, this bright red fire engine is the winery's mascot and can be seen during business hours in front of Hook & Ladder Winery. It has been admired and photographed by hundreds of visitors, including past and present members of the fire fighting team from Berkeley Heights, New Jersey.

PARADISE RIDGE WINERY

Besides being utilized every harvest, this 1962 Ford dump truck was used in a documentary film about the life and times of Kanaye Nagasawa. His biographical story was nationally televised in Japan.

In 1865, Nagasawa was smuggled out of Japan. His quest was to study Western science, which was strictly forbidden at the time. In Great Britain, he met utopian religious leader Thomas Lake Harris. Harris sent Nagasawa to Cornell University in New York to study viticulture, with hopes that a future community might prosper from his scholarly winemaking skills.

Harris would later select Nagasawa as one of his leaders to oversee and cultivate grapes at Harris's new Santa Rosa estate, known as Fountain Grove Ranch. It became one of the ten largest wineries in California and the first to export to Great Britain. Locally, Nagasawa was known as the "Wine King."

Eventually, Harris willed Nagasawa the entire 2,500 acres. Because of discriminatory Alien Land Laws that forbade Japanese nationals from owning land in California, Nagasawa was unable to leave the land to his heirs.

Paradise Ridge Winery honors Kanaye Nagasawa with a historical exhibit located in their tasting room. The winery also offers exceptional panoramic vistas of the Russian River Valley and a captivating sculpture exhibit in a grove of ancient oaks.

KENDALL-JACKSON WINE ESTATE

FULTON

Fanucchi Vineyards

Robert Rue Vineyard & Winery

FANUCCHI VINEYARDS

Old Blue is a true survivor of the '60s. From attending the '67 World Expo in Montreal, dodging hailstorms in South Dakota's Black Hills, escaping Yellowstone's devastating fire, to rockin' at Bay Area concerts, this 1966 Ford Econoline-Falcon emerged unscathed.

The Fanucchis ordered it new from the factory. It was the top end model, including the biggest engine Ford offered at the time – the new big, inline six-cylinder. In the back was one bench. Beneath the passenger doors was an automatic step which extended when the doors were opened. The seats were often removed to enable the maneuvering of fifty-pound wooden lug boxes into the field at grape picking time.

After only thirteen years of wear and tear, Old Blue was confined to vineyard use and abuse, including the planting of what is now California's only Trousseau

Gris field. Upon high school graduation, the Fanucchis' son Peter became Old Blue's new guardian. With all its original dents, scratches and touch up paint spots, he took on the task of restoration and painting. Peter fine tuned it like a Swiss watch, achieving over twenty miles per gallon, which exceeded new trucks of the time.

Consequently, the old Falcon went back to work transporting hundreds of cases of Trousseau Gris and Old Vine Zinfandel to fine restaurants up and down the state of California. At the Zinfandel Advocates and Producers Grand Tasting event, a large winery banner was stretched across Old Blue's side panel, seen by roughly ten thousand tasters. It is still used for hauling and helping friends move furniture – but it longs for one final rock concert.

ROBERT RUE
VINEYARD & WINERY

Burgermeister Beer & Ale Brewing Company was the first owner of this 1942 Chevrolet flatbed truck known as Truck #18. It was used to pick up hops from the Russian River Valley and deliver them to San Francisco. In 1956, Truck #18 was acquired by the previous owners of Robert Rue Vineyard to haul grapes to Asti Winery.

After the Rues obtained ownership of the property in 1973, they also became the grateful owners of Truck #18. It was used in the field for stacking boxes of grapes to be hauled to their winery. Five years later, the worn out flatbed quit running. Truck #18 was given a permanent resting place and prominent placement at Robert Rue Winery. It serves as a fond reminder of days gone by, and is one of the most photographed trucks in the area. Many visitors pose for photos beside it. They capture vivid memories of their wine experience in the Russian River Valley and Robert Rue's Winery.

WINDSOR

Martinelli Winery & Vineyards

MARTINELLI WINERY & VINEYARDS

Lee Martinelli's uncle purchased this 1954 Chevrolet dump truck new. It has hauled thousands of tons of apples and a few hundred tons of grapes. The apples were hauled from their Windsor orchards to Sebastopol canneries.

In the '60s, the Martinellis drove the '54 Chevy and a '38 International loaded with all their belongings, refrigerators, freezers and two children to Chico State College. Two years later, the trucking twosome moved them to UC Davis and eventually delivered them home to Sonoma County.

Equipped with a strong six-cylinder engine, a four-speed transmission and a two-speed rear differential, this hefty dump truck is still in service. It hauls grape pomace from winery to dump site. It has always been dependable and will forever remain in the Martinelli equipment family.

MARTINELLI WINERY & VINEYARDS

Another farm family member of Martinelli Winery is this 1947 Chevy flatbed one-and-a-half-ton pickup. It was purchased sixty-six years ago by Lee Martinelli's uncle, who bought two identical trucks with license plates one number apart. For decades, this husky flatbed hauled truckloads of apples to nearby canneries.

Near future plans include a complete restoration to original condition and color, as well as rebuilding of six-cylinder engine for display at the Martinelli Winery on River Road in Windsor.

DRY CREEK GENERAL STORE

HEALDSBURG

A.Rafanelli Winery

Del Carlo Winery/Teldeschi Vineyards

Hafner Vineyard

Jimtown Store

Lambert Bridge

Longboard Vineyards

Timber Crest Farms

West Wines

A.RAFANELLI WINERY

Beyond remarkable are A. Rafanelli Winery's striking team of grape hauling triplets. Not only a local anomaly, they may be the only matching set of three vintage grape haulers in the entire state of California and possibly the nation. Two of the 1945 Chevrolet flatbeds were purchased by Americo Rafanelli (second generation) from a local Healdsburg dealership in 1946. Throughout the '40s and '50s, they were used for hauling grapes, prunes and pears. Americo's son, Dave Rafanelli, later found the third identical truck and meticulously restored the threesome. They continue to work diligently in the vineyards, playing a crucial role in the wine making process.

For most of the year, the classic trio hibernates in a local storage facility. During harvest, they are driven to the family vineyard and methodically filled one by one. The first truck is loaded with nine bins of hand picked grapes and moved to the front of the vineyard road. The second truck is then heaped full and parked directly behind truck number one. After the third truck can hold no more, it pulls up behind the other two in an organized line. In single file, the quiet procession begins, as if choreographed.

Slowly they caravan through the curves of Dry Creek, past neighboring vineyards, autumn trees and across the timeworn Lambert Bridge. Carefully, they wind their way up the hill to A. Rafanelli Winery for unloading.

With empty beds, the triplets return to their home vineyard in unison, almost instinctively, to repeat the ritual until every last grape is gone.

DEL CARLO WINERY/ TELDESCHI VINEYARDS

Scooped right off the showroom floor in 1950 by Mike Teldeschi, Ray's dad, this GMC went straight to work. For the next fifty-five years, it delivered grapes every harvest. Nicknamed Old Red, it made many trips to San Francisco bringing freshly picked grapes to eagerly awaiting home winemakers. The GMC also serviced local wineries that purchased fruit from Teldeschi Vineyards. Eventually, Old Red only hauled locally. In 2005, it worked harvest for the last time.

Today, Old Red is employed to take visitors on scenic tours of the Teldeschi Home Ranch. The truck bed, once laden with grape bins, now holds hay-bale benches to offer panoramic seating for their guests as they tour the ranch and its hundred-year-old vineyards.

HAFNER
VINEYARD

Shortly after V-J Day (Victory over Japan), the Hafner family purchased this two-ton 1946 Ford flatbed. It is the only original piece of equipment remaining on the ranch since the Hafners took ownership in 1967. Its primary mission was to haul farm products. Until the early 1970s, it carried hundreds of lug boxes filled with prunes to the co-op drier in nearby Healdsburg. Eventually, prunes were replaced by grapes and transported to Sonoma County wineries.

Fitted with a dumping lift, this powerful work truck moved many loads of rock from a Mayacama Mountain quarry to build roads through the Hafners' Vineyard.

Now, it makes occasional parade appearances and assists in vineyard events, like Chardonnay picking parties.

JIMTOWN STORE

Racing down the road at a frantic pace, screaming sirens and traffic scattering, was a routine ride for this '55 firefighting Ford. Back in the mid '50s and into the '70s, it was used as an auxiliary fire truck in the Anderson Valley of Mendocino County.

Now, it takes up residence at the neighborly Jimtown Store, situated at the ninety-degree bend in the road, in the breathtaking Alexander Valley.

Upon reopening of the store in 1991, the fire truck was procured by the current store owner, mainly to haul construction materials, antiques and topsoil. Today, it is a food purveyor at the local farmers' market, carrying everything from bakery goods, to store spreads and drinks, including their coveted hibiscus tea. The faded '55 Ford is an iconic fixture and an admired mascot, printed on T-shirts and mugs inside the store.

LAMBERT BRIDGE

Tucked in the hills of the Dry Creek Valley, on a narrow country lane, stands the lush Lambert Bridge Winery with its overflowing gardens, several supersized dogs and one spectacular 1947 Ford flatbed.

This Ford was sold at a Healdsburg Hospital fundraiser back in 2005 with its original flathead motor. In 2012, it was totally stripped down and completely refurbished. Since then, it has become quite a tourist attraction. Most winery guests snap a picture in front of the truck or sitting in the bed. It is used solely for parades. Otherwise, it stands regally at the entrance of the Lambert Bridge Winery tasting room, welcoming all who enter.

LONGBOARD VINEYARDS

Cruising down a narrow ocean frontage road, surfboards overhead, Beach Boys blaring and a boardwalk in the rear view mirror – all seem to be images one conjures up when looking at a Woody.

In 1999, this 1951 Ford Country Squire Woody was purchased in Fort Bragg with no engine and barely any wood. A complete frame-off restoration was done over the next four years. Other than a modern engine and drive train, it is as close to the original as possible. The wood is rock hard American Maple, sourced and bent by Rick Mack (a Woody restoration legend). It took months to do the fitting, finish

sanding and varnishing. Wine Country gnats seem to love the smell of varnish and keep sticking to the final of twelve coats.

Rather than being for show, this Woody is a driver. In the early days of Longboard Vineyards, it was used to deliver wine to local accounts by Oded, the owner, winemaker, Big Kahuna and chief mischief coordinator. Surfers are the ultimate searchers, interacting with nature's forces and always seeking that "perfect" wave. Winemakers – pretty much the same.

TIMBER CREST FARMS

Hauling raisins from ranch to packing shed in the Fresno area was the job of this DB-8, one-ton 1928 Sterling flatbed. The owner of Timber Crest Farms purchased it in its present condition as an addition to what may be the largest collection of Sterling trucks in the country. His oversized shop in Healdsburg houses at least eight of these lovingly refurbished vehicles. An extensive collection of tarnished shells and corroding cabs border the back of his monstrous shop. They supply parts for his ongoing projects or future restorations, some of which take years to complete.

WEST WINES

Milk, milk and more milk. This old Ford has probably seen more milk than most of us have seen in a lifetime. That's what happens when you work at a dairy. Borden's Dairy purchased this 1932 Ford flatbed for their Petaluma dairy plant. It was operated exclusively inside the plant and never driven on a public road. In the late '50s, it was retired and stored at the plant until 1999, when it was sold at an auction. Not long after the sale, Bengt Akerlind acquired it. He had it carefully restored to almost original condition for use in parades and exhibitions.

With the opening of West Wines in 2010, Akerlind needed a sturdy, dependable winery truck. Instead of buying a new one, additional mechanical work was performed on the dairy Ford. Today, it is fully operational and used for hauling equipment, case-goods, grapes and barrels. On occasion, you may even spot it in a local parade. Mooooove over!

WINE COUNTRY LISTINGS

Napa County

Artesa Vineyards & Winery
1345 Henry Road
Napa

Benessere Vineyards
1010 Big Tree Road
St. Helena

Beringer Vineyards
2000 Main Street
St. Helena

Bouchaine Vineyards
1075 Buchli Station Road
Napa

Bremer Family Winery
975 Deer Park Road
St. Helena

Calistoga Lighted Tractor Parade
Calistoga Chamber of Commerce
Calistoga

Carneros Region
Schwarze Ranch
Napa

Chateau Montelena Winery
1429 Tubbs Lane
Calistoga

Far Niente Winery
1350 Acacia Drive
Oakville

Fleury Estate Winery
950 Galleron Road
Rutherford

Flora Springs Winery
1978 West Zinfandel Lane
St. Helena

Frog's Leap Winery
8815 Conn Creek Road
Rutherford

Laird Family Estate Winery
5055 Solano Avenue
Napa

Lava Vine Winery
965 Silverado Trail
Calistoga

Long Meadow Ranch Winery
738 Main Street
St. Helena

Napa Marina
1200 Milton Road
Napa

Nickel & Nickel Winery
8164 St. Helena Highway
Oakville

Oakville Pump Service, Inc.
7855 St. Helena Highway
Oakville

Peju Province Winery
8466 St. Helena Highway
Rutherford

Pope Valley Garage
5875 Pope Valley Road
Pope Valley

Pope Valley Repair & Towing
5875 Pope Valley Road
Pope Valley

Regusci Winery
5584 Silverado Trail
Napa

Reynolds Family Winery
3266 Silverado Trail
Napa

Road 31 Wine Company
Kent Fortner
Napa

Robinson Family Vineyards
5880 Silverado Trail
Napa

Rossi Vineyard
St. Helena Highway
St. Helena

Round Pond Estate Winery
875 Rutherford Road
Rutherford

Rutherford Grove Winery
1673 St. Helena Highway
St. Helena

Tank Garage Winery
1020 Foothill Boulevard
Calistoga

Trailside Inn
4201 Silverado Trail
Calistoga

Turnbull Wine Cellars
8210 St. Helena Highway
Oakville

Uptown Theatre
1350 3rd Street
Napa

V. Sattui Winery
1111 White Lane
St. Helena

V12 Vineyards
2001 Soda Canyon Road
Napa

Sonoma County

Annadel Estate Winery
6687 Sonoma Highway
Santa Rosa

A. Rafanelli Winery
4685 West Dry Creek Road
Healdsburg

Beltane Ranch
11775 Sonoma Highway
Glen Ellen

Benziger Family Winery
1883 London Ranch Road
Glen Ellen

B.R. Cohn Winery
15000 Sonoma Highway
Glen Ellen

Cornerstone Sonoma
23570 Arnold Drive
Sonoma

D'Argenzio Winery
1301 Cleveland Avenue
Santa Rosa

Del Carlo Winery/Teldeschi Vineyards
4939 Dry Creek Road
Healdsburg

Dry Creek General Store
3495 Dry Creek Road
Healdsburg

Fanucchi Vineyards
1440 Wood Road
Fulton

Fremont Diner
2698 Fremont Drive
Sonoma

Glen Lyon Winery
2750 John's Hill Road
Glen Ellen

Gundlach Bundschu Winery
2000 Denmark Street
Sonoma

WINE COUNTRY LISTINGS

Hafner Vineyard
4280 Pine Flat Road
Healdsburg

Hook & Ladder Winery
2134 Olivet Road
Santa Rosa

Jimtown Store
6706 Highway 128
Healdsburg

Kendall-Jackson Wine Estate
5007 Fulton Road
Fulton

Lambert Bridge
4085 West Dry Creek Road
Healdsburg

Longboard Vineyards
5 Fitch Street
Healdsburg

Lovall Valley Vineyards
Jim Stroupe
Sonoma

Martinelli Winery & Vineyards
3360 River Road
Windsor

Matanzas Creek Winery
6097 Bennett Valley Road
Santa Rosa

Mayo Family Winery
13101 Arnold Drive
Glen Ellen

Paradise Ridge Winery
4545 Thomas Lake Harris Drive
Santa Rosa

Robert Rue Vineyard & Winery
1406 Wood Road
Fulton

Sonoma Creamery
21750 8th Street East
Sonoma

Sorento Imports
455 West Napa Street
Sonoma

St. Francis Winery & Vineyards
100 Pythian Road
Santa Rosa

Timber Crest Farms
4791 Dry Creek Road
Healdsburg

West Wines
1000 Dry Creek Road
Healdsburg

TURNBULL
WINE CELLARS

MORELAND

Ford

V12
VINEYARDS

FORD

California
ROAD 31

LONG MEADOW RANCH
LMR

WOODENHEA

STERLING

Pinot Grigio
Sangiovese
Phenomenon

Benessere
Italy In Napa!
← ▮▮ 1/2 mile

ACKNOWLEDGEMENTS

Since the inception of this project, the entire process has been an adventurous journey filled with surprisingly uncanny circumstances that greatly assisted in the making of this book. It became definitive early on, that spiritual guidance was being offered generously. For that, I must thank my mother.

To Richard Rawlings, cinematographer extraordinaire and 2014 American Society of Cinematographers Lifetime Achievement Award winner; thank you. Your photographic expertise and classic truck knowledge were invaluable in the production of this book.

To my editor and friend Keri Brenner, I owe a huge thank you. Her grammatical guidance and patience to persevere to the very end went above and beyond. To her, I am extremely grateful.

For the creative and technical assistance from my book designer, Zoe Lonergan; thank you. Her flexibility and willingness to accommodate without hesitation became an enjoyable and productive collaboration.

Thank you to my family and friends who have been so patient and tolerant of my excessive truck talk and lack of participation over the past year. A special thank you goes to Ross Chandler, Don Downs, Loretta Gavin, Kelly Neuman and Dwnell Testa. Your unwavering support and encouragement are etched in my heart.

If it were not for the stellar group of Napa and Sonoma County truck owners (in some cases past owners), this book would not have been possible. Thank you to all of you! You are admirable group of hard-working, entrepreneurial individuals who love life, the land and its rich heritage – and who were kind enough to share a slice of it. It has been a great honor to meet each and every one of you. Your time, effort and belief in my vision made this dream come true. It truly took a village to bring this passion to fruition.

Lisa A. Harris